Savvy Caddie

GOLF SECRETS

Author David Lynn Sisler

Inspired by Eric G. Burstock

Savvy Caddie Golf Secrets
Copyright © 2023 David Lynn Sisler
All rights reserved.

Requests and correspondence may be submitted by email: davesisler@gmail.com

ISBN: 979-8-9859459-3-5 (print)
       979-8-9859459-4-2 (epub)

Illustrations by Kimberly Merritt
Editing, formatting, and design by ChristianEditingandDesign.com

DEDICATION AND ACKNOWLEDGMENTS

To the God of Abraham, Isaac, and Jacob, and to Jesus Christ, who saved my sinful soul.

To my wonderful wife, JoAnn, and my entire family.

Thank you to my long-time friend and business partner, Eric G. Burstock, for giving valuable technical help and encouragement throughout the writing of this book.

Thank you to my friend and golf partner, Andy Capoccia, who always looks after my physical well-being on the course.

Contents

Foreword

As I read this book I visualized scenes from some great golf movies like *Caddyshack*, *Tin Cup*, *The Greatest Game Ever Played*, *A Gentleman's Game*, and *Dead Solid Perfect*.

I love that David's teaching techniques come from the observations of a caddie. There are some good tips in this book. It's definitely a good and fun read. You'll learn something about the game of golf.

—MONTY GOFF, PGA Golf Professional

West Virginia Assistant Director,
Veterans Golf Association

PGA Head Golf Professional,
Cacapon Resort State Park, West Virginia

Ode to Golf

by Allan Berman

In my hand, I hold a ball
white and dimpled, rather small
Oh, how bland it does appear
this harmless looking little sphere.

By its size, I could not guess
the awesome strength it does possess
But since I fell beneath its spell
I've wandered through the fires of hell.

My life has not been quite the same
Since I chose to play this stupid game
It rules my mind for hours on end
A fortune it has made me spend

It has made me swear and yell and cry
I hate myself and want to die
It promises a thing called par
If I can hit straight and far

To master such a tiny ball
should not be very hard at all
But my desires the ball refuses
and does exactly like it chooses

It hooks and slices, dribbles and dies
and even disappears before my eyes
Often it will take a whim
to hit a tree or take a swim

With miles of grass on which to land
it finds a tiny patch of sand
Then has me offering up my soul
if only it would find the hole

It's made me whimper like a pup
and swear that I will give it up
And take a drink to ease my sorrow
but the ball knows I'll be back tomorrow![1]

(Punctuation honored as found in cross referencing.)

Introduction

6:00 a.m. Nobody will tee off for another two or three hours, but you have to get there early to sign up. If you're there early you may be among the first up. The caddies are called up in order. If you're lucky you might get in two rounds for the day.

At $.75 per bag, two bags (a double) will earn you $1.50 for nine holes or $3.00 for eighteen, plus a tip. If you get in thirty-six holes for the day, you make $6.00 plus tips.

Usually you get maybe a $1.00 tip.

When you're ten or eleven years old, caddying makes for a long day, especially if you have to peddle your bike three miles each way, across town and up and down hills.

Caddie life in the late 1940s and early 1950s was an adventure for preteens and teens who were not privileged and not at the country club to swim in the fancy pool or play tennis. Instead, we were sent to the bottom of the steep hill that met the creek, and we hung out there until we were called up to the clubhouse for our assignments. We didn't have a caddie shack.

While awaiting our turn there were arguments, fights, wrestling matches, and card playing among us. We had to man up and take our licks, be they verbal or physical. They made us tough. Mommies were not there to protect us.

We had our rituals. Newbies had to go through initiation: running the gauntlet and getting tossed into the creek was part of it, and nobody escaped. Nicknames and hazing were part of being accepted. It wasn't a place for wimps.

One thing we all had in common: we were from the poor side of town or the county.

Great lifetime friendships evolved, and through the years some amazing adults came from our ranks of caddies who had toughed it out. Business owners, teachers, athletes, soldiers, politicians, golf pros, and many success stories emerged from those ranks.

We learned many life lessons from being the

poor among the elite, including perseverance, communication, and the value of integrity; and we gained insight into good personal habits and behaviors.

The main point of this book is how to play and enjoy the game of golf.

(G) = glossary

CHAPTER 1

Caddie

There was a time when caddies were an important part of the golf game at the local country club. Everyone walked back then, and the caddie played an important role.

First, the caddie had a trained eye for locating and marking the landing spot of the player's ball, which most times was in the rough or the woods or near a hazard.

The caddie would also offer advice: which club was suitable for the next shot, the lay of the green, and the location of the trouble spots.

Most important, the caddie did the grunt work, cleaning the clubs and carrying the bag of clubs up and down the hills.

On a humorous note, one caddie was carrying

a local doctor's clubs and the good doctor hit one onto the side of a hill, which was overgrown with bushes and weeds. After they had searched for the ball quite a while, the doc asked the caddie, "Did you mark where the ball landed?" The caddie replied that he had, and the doctor asked, "Well, what did you mark it by?"

"A large black bird," replied the caddie.

Obviously, it wasn't a good day for the caddie. True story.

Local players were quite colorful in their clothing, actions, and language. Caddies got a good education.

Today few places use caddies, except for professional tours. Caddies had an educational experience because they saw it all. The better golfers gave them insight on the right way to hit a golf ball, and poor players showed them what not to do.

On designated slow days, usually Mondays, caddies with clubs were allowed to play golf. Many club members allowed caddies the use their clubs, a generous gesture.

I once played nine holes with the only club I had—a mended 5 iron I'd found. I drove, hit the second shot, chipped, and putted with it. Incidentally, I shot forty-five. Makes you wonder why we need all the modern equipment. Later a member allowed me to use his clubs on caddie day.

Some caddies learned to play very well without the benefit of lessons, relying on what they'd observed and learned from members who were good golfers.

The tips I give in this book are those I learned from club champions and local pros on hot, steamy summer days.

CHAPTER 2

Enjoying the Game

G olf, if taken too seriously, can bring out the worst in a person. Or it can be the challenge that teaches perseverance, patience, and humility.

Wanting to win and be the best is always a good thing, but there's only one winner and one best. Does that mean all the rest of us should stay home or sit in the clubhouse and drink beer? The simple answer is no. Golf should be an enjoyable outing that offers much to be appreciated:

- a personal challenge to make constant self-improvements

- a chance to develop friendships and associates and learn new things about life

- an exercise of body and mind

- a removal from cares of the world and your problems, even if temporary

- a chance to recognize your vulnerable areas and learn humility and other life lessons

- an opportunity to play together on a somewhat equal level because of the genius handicap system that makes playing fun for individuals and teams

- a chance to test your integrity and take pride in yourself as golf is a self-regulating honor system

- a chance once in a while to beat them "sumb#!@hes"

CHAPTER 3

Some Nitty-Gritty

I've been privileged to help a few people get started in playing golf, and I'd like to give you some tips that may help you, even if you've been playing for a while.

First, all young people have the mistaken idea that they have to hit a golf ball as hard as they can swing and make it go 300 yards. And the first thing they want to pull out of the bag is the driver.

I like to start a new player with just a 7 iron to develop consistency. A 7 iron is much easier to hit than a driver.

1. Hit the 7 iron only in the beginning.

2. Learn to hit it straight every time.

3. Then work on distance.

If you can hit it straight and 140 or 150 yards, work on consistency. Try to hit it 140 yards straight every time. Then you'll have the ability to swing other clubs.

Get good with that 7 iron and everything else will fall in line.

A common error that many new and skilled golfers make is trying to hit the ball too hard. They look at me in disbelief when I say—

"In order to get the ball to go long, you have to swing easy."

"In order to get the ball to go up, you have to swing down on it."

I know that sounds opposite of what you'd think, but it's the truth. A fluid swing that strikes the ball squarely will give you good distance. When you hit down on the ball, you pinch it against the earth, which causes the ball to leap into the air.

Reverse every natural instinct and do the opposite of what you are inclined to do, and you will probably come very close to having a perfect golf swing.[2]

—BEN HOGAN

As your ability grows through practice, you'll become longer, more accurate, and consistent. You can then learn things like shaping the flight of the ball and spinning it.

A club champion on the course where I worked took only a half backswing. The key to his success, even though he didn't hit the ball as far as others, was that his drive was always down the middle of the fairway.

Another part of his success was that his wedge play was extremely good. When he'd pull the wedge from the bag, I always knew he was going to be on the green with a makeable putt. He rarely posted a score above par.[G]

Caddie note: When the player went to the range to practice, guess which club he hit?

In those days the caddie would shag balls for the player, which meant standing in a field with a bag and picking up the balls as the player hit them. Some of us liked to catch balls on the fly with the bag. The player became so good with his wedge that we could almost stand in one spot to catch his practice shots.

The best golfer I knew at the time was an older

gentleman who never hit a drive over 175 yards. He was age sixty-five and a par golfer because of his driving accuracy and medal play.

The point:

Control is more important than distance for amateur golfers.

Professional golf is a little different because most professionals have already accomplished accuracy (to a degree) by the time they make the professional ranks. At that point, distance becomes a factor.

A primary difference between amateurs and professionals is reaching par 5 holes in two instead of three. And reaching par 4 holes in two with a wedge instead of a 5 iron is an advantage pros enjoy because of their driving distance. A wedge delivers more accuracy and is considered a "scoring iron."

Some casual golfers somewhat defeat themselves by playing from the wrong tee boxes. I've seen people playing from the tips (longest tee boxes) who cannot hit a golf ball two hundred yards.

The purpose of different tee boxes is to equalize the players. It's not a macho matter; you should always play from the tee boxes that are designed for your age and ability. Players who aren't capable of playing from the tips slow the game for the players behind them and frustrate themselves.

**Enjoying the outing is primary
to your golfing experience.**

Make it fun. Play with your current capability and learn from your experiences.

CHAPTER 4

Rules and Etiquette

Golf rules are essential for the integrity of the game in competitive play. If you're playing in a tournament, you should know the rules so everyone in your group is on an equal playing field.

No matter the circumstance, honesty is expected.

Primarily, rules are self-enforced, which is uniquely different from many other sports that need referees or judges to call the fouls or violations. In golf, if you do something against the rules, it's pretty much up to you to call it yourself. Although some people you play are "golf police," mostly your violations are on you to confess.

When you're playing with friends and you're all in agreement, some variances are acceptable.

The following makes the game a little more user friendly:

- **Mulligan**, sometimes referred to as a "breakfast ball," may be allowed after a bad tee shot on the first hole. Sometimes a group of players agree to allow one mulligan per round or one on each of the nine holes, anywhere, or only on a drive.

  Justification for a breakfast ball is that we're not professional golfers but on the course to enjoy our golf outing among friends.

  Pros, however, hit hundreds of balls before a round in order to warm up.

  Amateurs are usually rushing to make tee time, not hitting practice shots before the round. We're walking onto the first tee box cold, having not hit a golf ball since the last time we played. A mulligan is fair, giving us a chance, at least, to a good start.

- **Fluff the ball**[(G)] allows a player to move the ball a bit to improve his "lie."[(G)] Let us say you hit a very good tee shot down the middle of the fairway but unfortunately it comes to rest in someone's divot who failed to repair it. Casual golfers say the circumstance is unfair and undeserving of a penalty, even though you hit a good shot. Therefore, it's justifiable to move your ball a little.

Professional golfers are usually playing in pristine conditions. The fairways are like cushions and the course is well manicured. Most public courses are flawed, with nowhere near the immaculate conditions that professionals enjoy.

- **Gimmees** are much contested, but among friends it's not uncommon to give a putt to someone if the ball lies within a certain limit, predetermined and agreed upon by all involved—let's say "inside the leather." This refers to the distance between the putter head and where the grip starts. The net result is that the distance is the same for everyone, which speeds up play a bit.

There's a saying among players who call

for gimmees: "Even Ray Charles could make that putt."

These agreed-upon rule-benders make the game more enjoyable for casual golfers. After all, we're not out there to punish ourselves or aim for the U.S. Open. We're there to have fun, relieve stress, and get a little sun and exercise. Most charity tournaments, known as "captain's choice" or "scrambles," allow for these alterations of the rules.

There are certain rules of etiquette that everyone should understand and adhere to that are mostly common sense. But sometimes new golfers need to be advised so they'll know how best to take part:

- Do not walk in someone's line of putt.

- Repair your divots on the fairway and your ball marks on the green.

- Rake the sand trap for the players behind you.

- Do not drive your golf cart across tee boxes or too close to a green.

- When someone is putting, do not move, talk, cough, or fart during their backswing.

A kid grows up a lot faster on the golf course. Golf teaches you how to behave.[3]

—JACK NICKLAUS

CHAPTER 5

Some How-Tos

Tension is your enemy in the game of golf. Have you ever been sitting in your office and you wadded up a sheet of paper and casually tossed it across the room and landed it in the trash can? Then someone says, "I'll bet you can't do that again!" So you take the challenge. You wad up a piece of paper, take aim, toss it, and miss. The reason you missed is that you tensed up.

Forearm tension will cause problems with the natural flow of your golf swing.

Have you ever casually hit a putt one-handed across the green and made it in? Most of us have done that. But put another ball down and try to make the putt. What happens? You likely miss. Why? Because you tense up and either pull or push the putt. You allow your mind and body to overtake your instinct, which interferes with your hand-to-eye coordination.

Learn to relax your arms, breathe naturally, and get rid of tension before you make the stroke.

> **TIP:** You'll want to remember that a putt will break away from mountains or hills and toward bodies of water like lakes and rivers most of the time.

You've probably not heard that tip from a teaching professional.

There are some people who have natural athletic ability and many who don't. A baseball swing and golf swing have similarities: both require a good body turn and hand-to-eye coordination.

I like to start new players swinging a club like a baseball bat for them to get the feel of the turn and the torso rotation.

Gradually lowering the swing until your club is near the ground gets your body loosened up and into the proper swing motion.

If you have natural athletic ability, you'll

quickly adapt to hitting a stationary object on the ground. Don't complicate it. Just hit it.

For those who don't have natural athletic ability, you can still enjoy the game of golf! The difference is, you'll have to rely on a mechanical swing. Enlisting a professional instructor can help you form a swing that can be repeated and practiced.

A doctor I caddied for had no natural athletic ability, and he was left-handed and awkward. Caddying for him was an adventure for me. As time passed, the doc formulated a swing that worked for him, and even though he never became a "good" golfer, he was able to enjoy the game and he played regularly with his foursome.

Not everyone can become a professional golfer, but everyone can have fun and enjoyment from the sport.

> **When I swing at a golf ball right, my mind is blank and my body is loose as a goose.**[4]
>
> —SAM SNEAD

> **Grip the club as if you were holding a baby bird.**[5]
>
> —SAM SNEAD

CHAPTER 6

Putting

The golf ball is 1.68 inches in diameter and the hole is 4.25 inches wide. The point of putting is to roll the ball from where it rests on the green and get it into the hole with as few strokes as possible, normally two when trying to shoot par.

Most new golfers are fearless, and even though they typically hit the ball too hard, they make quite a number of putts. That's because they hit it straight at the hole; and because they hit it hard, they eliminate the "break" (the slant or roll of the green). If they miss the hole, they'll have a long putt coming back.

Gradually the new player will learn to finesse the ball or slow it and then he or she will need to learn how to read the green—observe the undulations, the bend of the grass, and the speed of the green.

Good putters are able to control the ball, so even if they miss the hole, the remaining putt will be a foot or less. Three putting (to make the hole) will too often ruin what could otherwise have been a good score for the round.

Every golfer should realize that if he or she putts in regulation, half of par for the course is used up in putts: 18 holes x 2 putts per green = 36 putts. Par for most courses is 70 or 72. So cutting your number of putts is crucial to posting a good score.

There's an old saying that makes a lot of sense: "Drive for show; putt for dough."

I like to set my goal at 30 putts per round to have a little room for error in my medal play,[G] also known as strokeplay.

You'll have good days and bad days putting—a fact of life and the sport. You'll just have to learn to live with the fact that some days you'll be "on" and other days you'll be "off."

I've often said that equipment is not a factor in

putting, though clubhouse pros will probably disagree because they want to sell you the latest and greatest. To be honest, I've probably made as many putts with a $5 yard sale putter as I have with my $400 Scotty Cameron. When you're seeing the putts and have the "feel," you could putt with a Coke bottle on the end of a stick and make the putts.

Women vs. Men

I believe women are better putters than men, generally. I'm not sure why they are, but they seem to have some kind of magic that makes their putting look easy.

Women also seem to have a little more patience than men and an intuition thing in their favor. Maybe they're able to interpret their intuition over a putt while men have to rely on their ability to read the break.

Another factor could be a woman's memory. She never forgets anything! She probably remembers her play from five years ago on a particular hole when the caddie told her, "The putt breaks four inches from left to right and straightens out two feet from the hole." If that putt comes up again, she's got it!

Women also seem more relaxed about a putt, and men are fidgety. Men will grip, re-grip, take several stances, and back off and look at it from all angles. Once again, tension is the enemy in putting. The more relaxed you are, the better you'll putt.

> **TIP:** Keep your head behind the ball. If your head moves, it means your body is swaying. Putting is arms only.

Put that in your memory bank.

The three things I fear most in golf are lightning, Ben Hogan, and a downhill putt.[6]

—SAM SNEAD

CHAPTER 7

The Second Shot

Ibelieve the second shot is the most important shot for any golf hole. Once the drive is hit, and if in play, the next shot is your most important.

If you're within range of the green, you want to try to get the ball there, of course. If not on, you want the ball to be in a position for an easy "chip"(G) and putt. You don't have to hit every green in regulation in order to make par. You can learn this by watching senior golfers. Many seniors can't hit the green in two strokes on a par 4. But they've adjusted to the game and become very good at positioning their second shot to easily chip it close and make the par putt.

The second shot on a par 3 hole is most

important because if you're on the green in one, you're "birdie putting."[G] If you're not on the green, you're chipping for position to make a par putt. So either way, the second shot is the most important.

On a par 5 hole, as a casual golfer you generally can't make the green in two. Therefore, the second shot is crucial to get the ball to a spot where you can get your third shot on the green.

Most of us have a "go-to" club we can hit with pretty well more often than not.

Let's say you're 240 yards out and you know you can't reach the green in two. This is where the importance of the second shot comes into play.

Many golfers play the second shot kind of dumb. They pull out a 3 wood, which is hard to hit to begin with, and swing as hard as they can. They either top it, pull it into the rough, or hit a "wormburner,"[G] which leaves the golfer in a bad position for his or her third shot.

Use your go-to club to position your second shot within 90 to 100 yards of the green. Then you'll have a great chance of getting it on the par 5 in three shots. This is called course management.

Stop playing dumb, trying to be Mr. Macho, and learn the value of a good second shot.

Again, my opinion is that the second shot on each hole, be it a par 3, 4, or 5, is the most important shot. Put that in your pea brain and try to remember it.

Placing the ball in the right position for the next shot is 80 percent of winning golf.[7]

—BEN HOGAN

CHAPTER 8

Hitting or Swinging

Some recreational players hit the golf ball as though they're striking it with a hammer and others swing smoothly and with balance.

Hitters typically have a very firm grip on the club and their trail hand (dominant hand) turned as far right (or left for left-handers) as they can. I call this the death grip.

A hitter will commonly pull the ball or at worst duck hook(G) it.

There's good reason a golf swing is called a *swing*.

My opinion is that people who learn to swing smoothly and with a neutral or slightly strong grip are the most consistent golf ball launchers.

Good golfers say that when they swing the club, the idea is to just let the ball get in the way. By perfecting a smooth, balanced, rhythmic swing, you can learn to groove it and the swing soon becomes natural and effortless in appearance.

If you observe how most professional female golfers swing, you would definitely conclude that most of them are swingers rather than hitters. The swings are usually smooth, very consistent, and look effortless. Yet they smack the ball longer than most men who are casual golfers.

Rather than trying to nail the ball like a carpenter would a nail, it may be wise for you to work on a good swing. Good examples are Fred Couples, Ernie Els, Sam Snead, and Annika Sorenstam.

If you have trouble by trying to overpower the ball with a choppy swing, try this exercise:

1. Tie a short rope to a bucket of water.

2. In your golf stance, as follows, swing the bucket back and forth.

   ○ The body begins to turn first,

   ○ then the hands pull through,

   ○ followed by the bucket of water.

3. As the arc widens, you'll feel the bucket begin to lag in the backswing. This is the feeling you want to develop in your golf swing. The lag is critical to a good swing.

4. Next, set the bucket down and grab your golf club.

   o Start your body turn at the top of the back swing,

   o followed by your hands,

   o with clubhead trailing.

Once you begin to feel the lag, you can develop a great club head speed as you release your hands, creating a whip motion—sort of like snapping a towel in the locker room.

The lag is where your power comes from, not from trying to crunch a ball with a strong grip and muscle power.

All the above is this old caddie's observation.

For myself and other serious golfers there is an undeniable beauty in the way a fine player sets his hands on the club.[8]

—Ben Hogan

CHAPTER 9

Chipping or Dipping

By chipping and dipping, I'm not talking potato chips and cheese dip, though I *am* going to talk "chili dip."

Professionals are good at using lofted wedges(G) from just off the green. But you must remember that they spend hours practicing chips and they play almost every day. For casual, amateur golfers who don't get much practice and maybe play only once or twice a week, it's almost impossible with a wedge to play well around a green. Instead, we almost always leave it short or "chili dip it"(G) and it goes nowhere.

Due to wrong club selection, many shots are lost around the green.

So what's the solution?

I suggest simply getting the ball rolling toward the hole instead of trying to chip it up.

- Avoid digging a wedge in the ground or sculling the ball across the green by blading it or hitting it on the leading edge of the club instead of the club face.

- If the grass is as tall as your ball, use a hybrid with a little loft.[G]

- If you don't have a hybrid club in your bag, a 3 wood is just as effective. Just shorten your grip a little, play the ball back in your stance a bit, with weight shifted to the front, and follow through.

  - If you're on the fringe, off the green, use a putter.

- Put most of your weight on your front foot, with a narrow stance, and swing through.

- Do not forget to take dead aim!

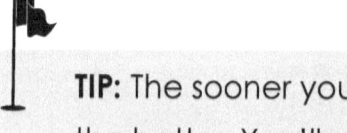

TIP: The sooner you can get the ball rolling the better. You'll save a lot of shots by not trying to hit pro shots with a wedge.

If there's some grass growth between the green and your ball but you have a clean shot, use this little trick:

Forward press* your putter, closing the face a little, and then just follow through with your putt.

*Lean your hands ahead of where the ball lies, creating a closed face on the putter.

When your arms swing the putter through, it crests and the ball will take a little hop with an overspin and just pop right through the grass to the green. Make sure you aim at the hole because the ball is going to go straight.

You can thank me when some of your golf buddies look at you with surprise and say, "How did you do that?!"

CHAPTER 10

Trash Talk, Humor, and Unsolicited Advice

Jabs

Opportunity for humor and trash talk abounds among recreational golfers enjoying friendships in a round of golf. Funny things happen out there, and humor and trash talk can become common in the comradery.

Don't poke fun when

- there's organized competition or money involved (most rounds of golf usually involve some sort of wager, either individually or by team play),

- you're playing with someone you don't yet know well,

- golfing with a client who's become a friend (he or she is always a client first, and there can be a fine line on the course between you and the client-turned-friend), and

- a player is concentrating on a shot to win or tie a hole for himself or herself or the player's team.

Among friends, also consider those who don't respond well to trash talk on the golf course.

TIP: Be self-aware and aware of others.

Among your regular foursome friends, some friendly barbs, humor, and trash talk may be common and even expected. With a group of male players, for instance, there may be a time when you come up short on a putt and someone pipes up, "Does your husband play too?" Or you may finally out-drive your better competitor, and as you pass by his ball you say, "Nice drive, Alice."

Friendly jabs among friends on a golf outing aren't uncommon before, during, and after a round. If you're the sensitive one, learn to laugh at yourself, learn to receive the jabs in the group's spirit of fun, and learn how to dish it out.

The bantering is a factor that makes golfing among friends so enjoyable and worthwhile. But always consider the circumstances and those you're golfing with.

Your default should be respect.

Unsolicited Advice

Regardless of who you're golfing with, offering golf advice is not a good practice. Advice should be reserved for when someone asks for help. Even then, limit the advice.

In most cases we each likely know what we and others are doing wrong in our plays, and few of us appreciate unsolicited advice. What's especially offensive is when the advice-giver is no better at golfing than the one getting the advice.

When someone asks for help, inviting advice, that's a different matter. If someone in your golfing group incessantly gives you unwanted advice, politely tell him or her that you'd rather figure it out yourself.

Do not be an unsolicited golf instructor.

> **If you can't laugh at yourself, then how can you laugh at anybody else?**[9]
>
> —PAYNE STEWART

CHAPTER 11

The Dreaded Slice

A "slice" occurs when your clubface is open at impact or when you swing across the ball from the outside inward instead of hitting it squarely on the clubface.

Most new golfers develop a slice on their drives and older golfers are typically plagued with this problem. It's a monkey on your back that's difficult to shake off.

It's common for a golfer to "come over the top"(G) or swing from the outside to the inside of thc setup. Overcoming these habits is hard, and most players try to adjust for the slice by playing for it instead of trying to correct it.

A common error is opening the stance and aiming down the left side of the fairway (if you play right-handed) or the right side (if you play left-handed). This error grows worse because the tendency is to open the stance farther and farther, trying to compensate.

The cure is to square the clubhead at impact and swing from the inside outward instead of outside inward or over the top.

If you've ever played ping-pong, you know how to cut the ball and put a sidespin on it: you either cut across the ball or uppercut the ball.

Similarly, the same principle applies to hitting a golf ball. When you observe professional players, notice that their trail elbow is always near their hip or touching their hip as they swing through.

By keeping your elbow in, you can't help but swing a bit from the inside outward. This habit, along with a squared clubface, will create a straight shot or slight draw. Many players consider a slight draw as optimal because they experience a better rollout, which means a longer distance.

Only with practice over time will your proper swing habit become natural for you. A good teaching pro can help you groove a swing that works for you.

TIP: Get rid of the slice because it's a distance killer, and no matter how much you try to play for it, it'll only get worse for your game.

CHAPTER 12

Pick a Target

With all due respect given for instinctive shooters, most of us are not that blessed. We need to aim. Marshall Dillon (*Gunsmoke* series) could quick draw and hit his target every time, but that was in the wilds of TV. It's hard to experience success at anything without a specific goal. The same principle applies to golf. Without a specific target, it's difficult to be successful.

Many golfers approach a tee shot just trying to hit it out there into the yonder. The result is most likely that the drive will not go where you'd like it to land.

You must pick a target for every shot in golf.

When you approach your tee shot with a driver in hand, you need to know exactly where you intend to hit the golf ball. Always pick a specific target spot to aim for. You'll be surprised how often your subconscious then takes over, and then your body responds, and you hit your target.

If you get up there just hoping to make good contact, it's likely not going to go well.

When you play darts, basketball, billiards, or pitch horseshoes, you have a target you're focused on. When you play golf, your aim is the green, but with a specific landing spot. Too many times casual golfers shoot in the general direction of their goal without considering the result.

Before you hit the ball, you must visualize the specific spot on the green where you want your ball to land.

Bunkers, water, trees, and other such course hazards are where you'll be severely penalized if you're slightly off with your shot. Mean, ornery, devious characters—greenskeepers— took great delight in planting holes directly behind hazards, leaving you little room for error. Where hazards appear, you'll need to use your head for something other than a hat rack. Unless you're Phil Mickelson or Tiger Woods, avoid those "sucker pin"(G) placements!

Go for the wide part of the green and aim for a specific spot with the idea of two putting. This approach will save you many strokes in the long run. Again, I must emphasize that every shot requires a target. Famous golf teacher Harvey Penick often said, "Take dead aim!"[10]

Before hitting your drive, look at the fairway in front of you and pick a tree, a bush, or a particular spot in line with where you want your ball to go. Where I couldn't see the fairway from the tee box, I've even lined up with a still or slow-moving cloud.

Always choose some kind of target to aim at.

Take that advice and you'll be surprised how many times you land the ball exactly where you aimed. You'll be patting yourself on the back as you walk down the fairway to high-five your ball.

For your approach to the second shot, strategize the location that's to your best advantage when your ball lands and comes to rest.

- If you're going for the green, choose exactly where you want the ball to land and aim at that target.

- If you're hitting for position on your next shot, pick the exact spot you want the ball to land, and then execute with confidence.

When you're putting, read the putt—find the line and pace of the putt—and then pick a spot between your ball and the hole where you want the ball to roll across. The spot should be just a foot or two in front of you. You can choose an irregularity or brown spot—anything to aim at that's in direct line with where you want the ball to roll.

It's easier to hit a spot shorter than to just aim right or left of the hole according to the break. Then just relax your tension and roll it.

The point: you must have a specific target on every shot. As I said, use your head for something besides a hat rack.

CHAPTER 13

Do the Math

Visualize the straight and level stretch of an interstate highway that's 3.5 miles long, or the length of a golf course, 6,200 yards. As an example, use the white tees on this scorecard.

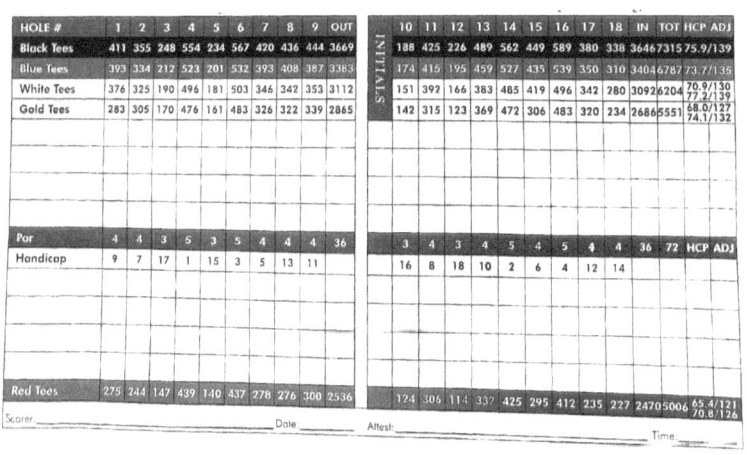

HOLE #	1	2	3	4	5	6	7	8	9	OUT		10	11	12	13	14	15	16	17	18	IN	TOT	HCP ADJ
Black Tees	411	355	248	554	234	567	420	436	444	3669		188	425	226	489	562	449	589	380	338	3646	7315	75.9/139
Blue Tees	393	334	212	523	201	532	393	408	387	3383		174	415	195	459	527	435	539	350	310	3404	6787	73.7/135
White Tees	376	325	190	496	181	503	346	342	353	3112		151	392	166	383	485	419	496	342	280	3092	6204	70.9/130 77.2/139
Gold Tees	283	305	170	476	161	483	326	322	339	2865		142	315	123	369	472	306	483	320	234	2686	5551	68.0/127 74.1/132
Par	4	4	3	5	3	5	4	4	4	36		3	4	3	4	5	4	5	4	4	36	72	HCP ADJ
Handicap	9	7	17	1	15	3	5	13	11			16	8	18	10	2	6	4	12	14			
Red Tees	275	244	147	439	140	437	278	276	300	2536		124	306	114	337	425	295	412	235	227	2470	5006	65.4/121 70.8/126

Scorer _____ Date _____ Attest: _____ Time _____

Image from Blue Ridge Shadows Golf Club, Front Royal, VA

You're going to hit your driver 14 times. To play for par in regulation, most golf courses have the following holes:

> 4 par 3 holes —up to 200 yards, usually
>
> 4 par 5 holes — 450 to 600 yards
>
> 10 par 4 holes — 240 to 490 yards

That's a total of 72 strokes for par.

Golf courses range from 70 to 72 for par, and courses may vary in the number of par 3 and par 5 holes. The following calculation is to shoot par 72 in regulation.

> Shooting par allows for 36 putts, 2 per hole.
>
> That's 14 drives with 22 shots, other than driver or putter.
>
> Therefore, you must cover 3.5 miles or 6,200 yards in 36 strokes—an average of approximately 172 yards per stroke.
>
> So depending on how far you can hit your driver, you can figure the length of your remaining strokes.

Driver hit: **Average second shot to the green:**

Driver hit:	Average second shot to the green:
200 yards	156 yards
225 yards	131 yards
250 yards	106 yards
275 yards	81 yards
300 yards	56 yards

On a par 5 hole, second shot:

Driver hit:	Average second shot to the green:	2 shots:
200 yards	295 yards	150
225 yards	270 yards	135
250 yards	245 yards	125
275 yards	220 yards	110
300 yards	195 yards	100

These shots vary, of course, by the actual length of the hole you are playing.

Use your head and do not mess with the 3 wood. It's probably the hardest club in the bag to hit and there are times to use it. For example, when you're playing in a captain's choice tournament, you may need the 3 wood to help get your team in a good position for the third shot on a par 5.

Now consider these points:

- Imagine the golf course is straight, level ground for 3.5 miles—no trees, bunkers, water hazards, or hillside slopes to consider—you have only one primary consideration: hit the ball straight. Just get on the tee box and hit the ball straight down the field.

- If your mind can disregard all obstructions on the course—you're only picking a target and hitting the ball there—how will this focus affect your golf game?

Golf is pretty much a mental game.

Once you have a reliable golf swing, the only thing between you and a good score is your mental attitude.

If you can imagine the golf course simply as yards to cover and eliminate the distractions, concentrating on just hitting the ball down the field as though you're on the driving range, you'll be able to conquer the course!

Remember this: the mechanics of a good golf swing do not change. If you can hit one good shot, you should be able to repeat that (in theory). Controlling your mind makes the difference.

When people say that golf is a game of inches, they're usually speaking about an errant putt that came up just short or barely missed to the right or left. But in the real world what matters most is those few inches between your ears, every time.

CHAPTER 14

The Real Challenge

The adversary is not the player or other players in your group. They're your friends and associates even when you're playing for a little money or just for bragging rights.

The real adversary is the *golf course*. It's like a puzzle or riddle you must solve to conquer the course. The course presents you with obstacles and visual challenges you must solve and overcome. It's you against the course, not against the players.

Once you realize you're at war with the course, not the players, you'll be in the right mindset.

Each hole has its own particular challenge. The course is on defense and you're always on offense, so strategizing your plays to beat the course is essential.

Incidentally, when you do well against the golf course, you'll likely collect a few bucks from the other players!

A good offense strategy for defeating the course is to play for par. There's a difference between playing for par and being too aggressive by playing for a birdie on every hole.

Remember the mean greenskeepers. The golf course was designed to trick you into taking low-percentage shots to go for birdies.

- Be careful about pin placements and strategically placed bunkers.

- Trees are not left standing on a golf tract by accident; they're obstacles to be overcome.

Though the course is designed to punish you, even if you slightly mishit a shot, you'll be tempted to go for it. Don't.

1. Think about the hole.

2. Strategize.

3. Force yourself to observe the consequences of a miss.

Playing for par sometimes means

- a layup and making a good pitch[G] or chip, or

- lagging a putt while seeking a birdie instead of being aggressive and ending up with a long comeback putt for par and ending up with a dreaded bogey.[G]

TIP: Whenever you get opportunities to play with better golfers, always do.

Sometimes you just need to see plays in real time to know certain things are possible. Playing with better golfers will help you pick up valuable pointers for your game. In addition, hitting some good shots will build your confidence.

Always be willing to learn and don't take yourself too seriously.

Learn to laugh at yourself when your attempts at play turn out silly. You're not aiming to become a tour professional, so don't lose friends because you expect so much from yourself on the course that you become irritable or angry with yourself and display that by throwing or breaking clubs. Take a chill pill and lighten up. It's just a game!

Besides, when you get so serious, you're sabotaging your game further because you're tensing up. Remember that tension is your biggest enemy in the golf swing.

CHAPTER 15

The Elusive Ace

In all the years I caddied, hundreds of rounds worked, I'd never witnessed a hole in one.

Until I finally made one myself.

A lot of aces are accidental and mishits.

My hole in one happened to be a nice 5-iron shot from an elevated tee box—across water. It hit just short of the pin and rolled into the hole.

A couple of years later, playing in a tournament, I hit a nice 5 wood shot that hit in front of the pin and rolled into the hole.

Those were the only two aces I'd ever witnessed in all my years as a caddie and player.

A semi-regular golfer in our group of friends was an average mid-handicap player who was a sort of frustrated athlete. He thought he should be a lot better. Whenever he hit a poor shot, he exhibited a lot of frustration, always complaining, "I'm better than that!"

I wasn't there on the day he topped his tee shot on a short par 3 hole and the ball kept rolling until it got to the green and then rolled across and went into the hole. A lousy golf shot turned into a hole in one.

All that is to say: many aces are pure luck. Nonetheless, it counts and goes on the record as a hole in one.

I know people who have four or five aces to their credit, mostly by luck. Of course, your chances are better if you consistently hit the par 3 greens with your tee shot.

An ace usually comes when least expected.

Good luck!

CHAPTER 16

The Last Putt

Youth today will probably never know the role of a country club caddie because of the advent of the motorized golf cart. The need for caddies has all but disappeared.

Clubhouse members no longer need to rely on someone to carry their clubs, which is kind of a shame. Youngsters who are growing up poor, as I did, no longer hang out at the local golf course and learn the way we did.

Back then a youngster had only a few choices for working and making a few dollars. The guys I knew either chased pins at the local bowling alley, ran a newspaper route, or caddied. Most of those have gone the way of the buggy whip—disappeared. In some locations in that generation there were summer jobs picking fruit or working on a farm.

Kids nowadays miss out on the early-morning fog, dew on the grass, the glory of sunrise, and the smell of the many flowers on the golf course.

They likely don't hear the frogs croaking along the creek or swat at mosquitoes or get caught in the sting of itchweed growing along the creek bed as they hunt for lost balls. A ball bearing a member's name earned us a dime at the pro shop.

Most kids today likely haven't had mud ball battles or cut the cover off a golf ball to unwind the rubber to find out what's in the center.

They've likely not experienced being thrown into a creek or fighting or wrestling to prove they're not cowards. I like the fact that we overcame our bullies.

Once grown up, they likely don't have lifetime friends with those they fought against in grass, under the sun, by the creek.

Along the way we caddies learned great lessons in humility, honesty, work ethics, and how to be gentlemen.

We also learned the game of golf from the ground up, which has served us well in our later years of life.

Be sure to see your local teaching professional for correct mechanical golf swing technique, instruction, and proper fitting for equipment.

Caddie note: You really can't putt that well with a Coke bottle on the end of a stick (chapter 6).

Finally, remember this:

TIP: Pick a target on every shot and use your head for something besides a hat rack.

If a guy is a good athlete, he'll end up being a pretty decent golfer if he just takes it up. But you never master it; even the best players in the world never master the game.[11]

—JACK NICKLAUS

My Golf Ditty

by David Sisler

My swing is not a problem
The shots fly straight and true
But aches and pains affect me
Before the game is through

Arthritis is the culprit
Each joint in me that moves
Makes it hard to swing the club
And hit it on the grooves

Tylenol nor alcohol
Can take the pain away
But winning always cures it
And that is why I play

Old Arthur tries to beat me
Each time I play the course
But victory is mental
An overcoming force

So off I go each golf day
To overcome two foes
The guys who want to beat me
And 'Ritis when he shows.

2012

Glossary of Terms

Birdie putt: usually one putt into the hole

Bogey: one over par

Break: degree a ball moves right or left in response to ground surface angles

Chili dip: mishit chip shot

Chip: short or low shot along the ground

Duck hook: ball turns sharply right or left

Fluffy lie: ball sitting atop the grass

Hybrid: wood or iron club

Lie: how the ball is sitting in the grass

Loft: angle formed between the clubface and ground

Lofted wedge: short-hitting club

Medal play: total strokes a player takes to complete a round

Over the top: overuse of upper body on the downswing

Par: the score standard for each hole

Pitch: a play into the green from typically 40-50 yards and closer

Sucker pin:	flagstick indicating risk factors like a bunker, water, drop-off
Tips:	longest tee boxes
Wormburner:	ball barely gets off the ground or doesn't at all
S#!t:	a common word heard often on a golf course

Endnotes

1. Allan Berman, "Ode to Golf," Fore All Things Golf, November 10, 2018, http://www.foreallthingsgolf.com/2184—2.

2. Jim Apfelbaum, *The Gigantic Book of Golf Quotations: Thousands of Notable Quotables from Tommy Armour to Fuzzy Zoeller* (New York: Skyhorse Publishing, 2007), 329.

3. Ibid., 253.

4. Virginia Golf Hall of Fame, accessed April 5, 2023, https://www.virginiagolfhalloffame.com/inductees/sam -snead/.

5. Kyle Shay, "Grip Strength Correlations to Speed," SuperSpeed Golf, November 30, 2022, https://superspeedgolf .com/blogs/news/grip-strength-correlations-to-speed.

6. Jim Apfelbaum, *1,001 Pearls of Golfers' Wisdom: Advice and Knowledge, from Tee to Green* (New York: Skyhorse Publishing, 2015), 75.

7. Ben Hogan Quotes, accessed April 10, 2023, https:// www.the-golf-experience.com/ben-hogan-quotes.html.

8. Ben Hogan and Herbert Warren Wind, *Ben Hogan's Five Lessons: The Modern Fundamentals of Golf* (New York: Atria Books, 1990), 18.

9. Apfelbaum, *The Gigantic Book of Golf Quotations*, 152.

10. Harvey Penick and Edwin Shrake, *The Wisdom of Harvey Penick: Lessons and Thoughts from the Collected Writings of Golf's Best-Loved Teacher* (New York: Simon & Schuster Paperbacks, 2015), 46.

11. "Jack Nicklaus's Interview on ESPN 980 Live from the Creighton Farms Invitational with Co-Hosts Chris Cooley and Kevin Sheehan," Nicklaus Design, September 15, 2016, https://www.nicklausdesign.com/2016/09/15 /jack-nicklaus-interview-espn-creighton-farms -invitational-hosts-chris-cooley-kevin-sheehan/.

Bibliography

Apfelbaum, Jim. *The Gigantic Book of Golf Quotations: Thousands of Notable Quotables from Tommy Armour to Fuzzy Zoeller.* New York: Skyhorse Publishing, 2007.

------. *1,001 Pearls of Golfers' Wisdom: Advice and Knowledge, from Tee to Green.* New York: Skyhorse Publishing, 2015.

Ben Hogan Quotes. Accessed April 10, 2023. https://www.the-golf-experience.com/ben-hogan-quotes.html.

Berman, Allan. "Ode to Golf." Fore All Things Golf, November 10, 2018. http://www.foreallthingsgolf.com/2184—2.

Hogan, Ben, and Herbert Warren Wind. *Ben Hogan's Five Lessons: The Modern Fundamentals of Golf.* New York: Atria Books, 1990.

"Jack Nicklaus's Interview on ESPN 980 Live from the Creighton Farms Invitational with Co-Hosts Chris Cooley and Kevin Sheehan." Nicklaus Design, September 15, 2016. https://www.nicklausdesign.com/2016/09/15/jack-nicklaus-interview-espn-creighton-farms-invitational-hosts-chris-cooley-kevin-sheehan/.

Penick, Harvey, and Edwin Shrake. *The Wisdom of Harvey Penick: Lessons and Thoughts from the Collected Writings of Golf's Best-Loved Teacher.* New York: Simon & Schuster Paperbacks, 2015.

Shay, Kyle. "Grip Strength Correlations to Speed." SuperSpeed Golf. November 30, 2022. https://superspeedgolf.com/blogs/news/grip-strength-correlations-to-speed.

Virginia Golf Hall of Fame. Accessed April 5, 2023. https://www.virginiagolfhalloffame.com/inductees/sam-snead/.

About the Author

David "Sonny" Sisler was born in Wardensville, West Virginia, in 1938. For his father's employment, the family moved to the small Southern town of Winchester, Virginia, where he grew up. Sonny is the oldest of four children.

As a young boy in the late 1940s, David worked as a country club caddie. In the early 1950s he was earning his own spending money and buying his school clothing.

In high school David played basketball and ran track and field. For basketball he was offered a partial scholarship to college, but he chose a different college and accepted the help of a Lions Club scholarship. After a year of college he dropped out and got a job.

David learned to play golf as a caddie, and the game stuck with him through life. He was always a fairly skillful player but had no opportunity to improve his ability in high school or college because there was no golf program.

Nevertheless, he maintained his skills and continued to play as a recreational golfer while raising a family and thereafter.

At this writing David is age eighty-four. Since the age of seventy-two he's continued shooting his age each year and said, "It's getting easier."

The tips and observances shared in *Savvy Caddie Golf Secrets* are not the end-all and should be used as guidelines in your pursuit of satisfactory recreational golf games.